BiBLE Activities in a SNAP

Bible Stories Come to Life

Rainbow Publishers®

www.rainbowpublishers.com

BIBLE ACTIVITIES

IN a

SNAP

Bible Stories Come to Life

WRITTEN AND ILLUSTRATED
BY BARBARA RODGERS

Dedication
To my husband, Rich: thanks for your love and support!

BIBLE ACTIVITIES IN A SNAP—BIBLE STORIES COME TO LIFE
©2009 Rainbow Publishers, twelfth printing
ISBN 10: 1-885358-42-3
ISBN 13: 978-1-885358-42-4
Rainbow reorder #RB36811
RELIGION / Christian Ministry / Children

Rainbow Publishers
P.O. Box 261129
San Diego, CA 92196
www.rainbowpublishers.com

Certified Chain of Custody
Promoting Sustainable
Forest Management
www.sfiprogram.org

SUSTAINABLE
FORESTRY
INITIATIVE

Author and Illustrator: Barbara Rodgers

Scriptures are from the *Holy Bible: New International Version* (North American Edition), copyright ©1973, 1978, 1984 by the International Bible Society. Used by permission of Zondervan Bible Publishers.

Printed in the United States of America

Contents

continued on next page…

Introduction

Welcome to *Bible Activities in a Snap*, a unique book series intended to bring joy, satisfaction and biblical understanding to children ages 3-8. Sunday school teachers, children's church leaders, Christian school teachers and home school parents will find this book series helpful for:

✳ reinforcing Bible lessons

✳ teaching spiritual concepts and biblical truths

✳ inspiring children's creativity

✳ providing lesson extension materials

This exciting concept offers two pages per lesson. For younger or less-skilled students, the left-hand page offers a finished illustration ready to color. The right-hand page of the same lesson is partially illustrated, allowing older or advanced children to use their imaginations and complete the scene. And because the pages are reproducible, you can duplicate the sheets to expand your curriculum, then allow the children to select the activity level they prefer. Every page includes a short narration and Scripture verse, so *Bible Activities in a Snap* may complement a lesson or serve as lessons themselves, making preparation truly a snap!

Here are some tips to get the best results from *Bible Activities in a Snap*:

✳ The pages are perforated for easy tear-out. However, you may want to copy them directly from the book to keep the lessons organized.

✳ When photocopying a page, place a sheet of black construction paper on the back of the original so the copier will not duplicate any print from the reverse side.

✳ Try offering different media for coloring, such as crayons of all shapes and colors, markers, colored pencils, chalk, paint and glitter pens.

✳ Show how to enhance some of the pictures by gluing basic elements to them such as yellow yarn for straw or cotton balls for sheep.

✳ Give the children additional instructions for drawing on the illustrations, or challenge the kids to devise their own one-of-a-kind work. There is no limit to the teaching and learning possibilities!

✳ Consider using the sheets as take-home pages for parental review so families may reinforce the lessons at home.

These books are so easy to duplicate and use that your only requirement is the desire to touch the hearts of young children with God's Word. Watch your children grow spiritually as God's precious Word is impressed upon their hearts and minds knowing "that your labor in the Lord is not in vain." (1 Corinthians 15:58)

GOD'S CREATION

God's creation is filled with many wonderful things. But most importantly God created people to live in the beautiful world He made. God created everything!

In the beginning God created the heavens and the earth. Genesis 1:1

ADAM AND EVE

God told Adam and Eve to eat the fruit from all of the trees in the Garden of Eden, except one. Satan became a snake and talked Eve into eating from that tree. Adam ate some, too. God was very unhappy with Adam and Eve because they did not obey Him. Draw some fruit on the tree and draw a snake wrapped around the tree.

When the woman saw that the fruit of the tree was good for food and pleasing to the eye, and also desirable for gaining wisdom, she took some and ate it. Genesis 3:6

NOAH AND THE ARK

Because the world was filled with evil people, God sent a flood to destroy everything. God told Noah to build a large boat called an ark and fill it with animals. Noah, his family and all of the animals were safe during the flood because Noah obeyed God.

Noah did everything just as God commanded him. Genesis 6:22

NOAH'S RAINBOW

After Noah's family and the animals came out of the ark onto dry land, Noah thanked God for keeping them safe. He built an altar and offered a sacrifice. God was pleased with Noah. He promised Noah that he would never destroy the earth **again** with a flood. He made a rainbow to remind us of this promise. Draw a **rainbow** coming out of the clouds and touching the hillside.

I have set my rainbow in the clouds. Genesis 9:13

Hagar Cries in the Desert

Hagar was alone in the desert with her son, Ishmael. Abraham sent her to the desert with some food and a container of water. After they used what they had, there was nowhere to get food and water. Hagar was afraid her son was going to die without water, so she put him under a shady bush. She kept watch over him from a distance. Ishmael was very thirsty and began to cry. Hagar was very afraid, and she began to cry, too. But God heard their cries.

And as she sat there nearby, she began to sob. Genesis 21:16

HAGAR FINDS WATER

Have you ever been so afraid that you cried? Hagar and Ishmael were afraid, and they cried. However, when Hagar looked up she saw a well of water. God had heard their cries. He knew what they needed. Hagar ran and filled her container with water. Now she and her son, Ishmael, would not die in the desert! Draw stones on the well that God provided for them.

Then God opened her eyes and she saw a well of water. Genesis 21:19

Rebekah Makes a Stew

Rebekah was the mother of Esau and Jacob. She favored Jacob and wanted his father Issac to give Jacob the family's blessing instead of Esau. Rebekah helped Jacob trick his father, Isaac, by making him a delicious meal. While Rebekah was cooking, Esau was out hunting so he could prepare his own meal for his father and receive the blessing. But Rebekah and Jacob had another plan.

I can prepare some tasty food for your father, just the way he likes it. Genesis 27:9

JACOB LIES TO HIS FATHER

Jacob lied to his sick and blind father, Isaac, by pretending he was his brother, Esau. He wanted the blessing that Esau was supposed to get. To fool his father, Jacob wore his brother's clothes and brought his father the tasty stew that Rebekah had made. He even put animal fur on his arms because Esau was a hairy man. Isaac didn't believe Jacob was really Esau until he felt his hairy arms. Isaac ate the stew and gave Jacob the blessing instead of Esau. Draw animal fur on Jacob's arms.

When Isaac caught the smell of his clothes, he blessed him. Genesis 27:27

JACOB'S COAT

Jacob had twelve sons but he loved Joseph the most. Jacob made Joseph a very colorful coat. Joseph's brothers were jealous of Joseph because of his father's favor toward him.

He made a richly ornamented robe for him. Genesis 37:3

JOSEPH, RULER OF EGYPT

When Joseph was the ruler of Egypt, ten of his brothers came to him to buy food for their families. The brothers did not know this ruler was Joseph because many years before they had sold him to a traveling merchant. But Joseph knew his brothers. He forgave them and gave them food and land. Draw one or more of Joseph's brothers as they talk to him on the throne.

You intended to harm me, but God intended it for good to accomplish what is now being done, the saving of many lives. Genesis 50:20

MOSES IN THE BASKET

When Moses was a baby, his mother hid him from Pharaoh. Pharaoh had declared that all boy babies should be killed. She placed Moses inside a basket she made and carefully set it in the reeds on the Nile River. When Pharaoh's daughter came to bathe in the Nile, she saw the basket and sent a slave to get it. Moses grew up in the palace as Pharaoh's grandson!

She named him Moses, saying, "I drew him out of the water." Exodus 2:10

MOSES, AARON AND PHARAOH

God sent Moses and Aaron to tell Pharaoh to let the Israelites go. Pharaoh did not want to release the Israelites because they were his slaves. To show Pharaoh God's power, God turned Aaron's staff into a snake. Pharaoh's magicians turned their staffs into snakes, too, but Aaron's snake swallowed theirs. God proved His power! Draw Aaron's snake swallowing the magicians' snakes.

Aaron's staff swallowed up their staffs. Exodus 7:12

PHARAOH AND THE FROGS

To convince Pharaoh to let the Hebrews leave Egypt, God caused ten plagues. One of these was a plague of frogs. Frogs covered all of the land in Egypt. They were everywhere! There was no place in Egypt that was not jumping with frogs. But as bad as the frogs were, Pharaoh still would not allow the Hebrews to leave Egypt. It took all ten plagues to convince him to let them go.

Their land teemed with frogs, which went up into the bedrooms of their rulers. Psalm 105:30

THE ANGEL PASSES OVER

The last plague was the plague of death of the firstborn son. To protect the Hebrews from this plague, God told them to put lambs' blood on the tops and sides of their doors. The angel of the Lord passed over the homes with the lambs' blood and the Hebrews were safe. Draw the angel passing over the Hebrew homes. Draw a child in one of the windows.

He will see the blood on the top and sides of the doorframe and will pass over that doorway. Exodus 12:23

21

MOSES AND THE RED SEA

When Moses led God's people out of Egypt they camped near the Red Sea. Pharaoh's army was coming after them and they had nowhere to go. But God was faithful and divided the sea waters so the Hebrews could cross on dry land to the other side.

Then Moses stretched out his hand over the sea, and all that night the Lord drove the sea back with a strong east wind and turned it into dry land. Exodus 14:21

WATER FROM THE ROCK

Moses led the Israelites through the desert. They camped at a place named Rephidim. The people complained because there was no water to drink. God told Moses to strike a rock with his staff. Miraculously, water gushed forth. God was faithful to the Israelites. Draw the water coming out of the rock.

Strike the rock, and water will come out of it for the people to drink. Exodus 17:6

A GOLDEN CALF

While Moses was on the top of Mt. Sinai receiving God's laws, the Israelites grew tired of waiting for him. Without their leader, they soon forgot that God brought them out of Egypt. Using gold jewelry, Aaron made a golden calf statue. They worshipped the idol with a big party.

He took what they handed him and made it into an idol cast in the shape of a calf. Exodus 32:4

MOSES AND THE TEN COMMANDMENTS

God called Moses to the top of Mt. Sinai where He gave him laws for living. The Ten Commandments were part of these laws. Exodus 31:18 tells us that God wrote the Ten Commandments on two stone tablets. These commandments were given to help the people live a life that pleases God. We still follow them today! Draw the stone tablets in Moses' hands.

Moses turned and went down the mountain with the two tablets of the Testimony in his hands. Exodus 32:15

RAHAB AND THE SCARLET CORD

Joshua, the leader of the Israelite army, was planning an attack on Jericho. The city of Jericho had high walls all around it so Joshua sent two spies to investigate. The spies stayed with a woman named Rahab in Jericho. Because she trusted God, she risked her life to hide the spies. They promised Rahab she would be safe during the attack if she put a scarlet cord in her window. When Joshua's army attacked Jericho, Rahab and her family were spared.

She tied the scarlet cord in the window. Joshua 2:21

JOSHUA AND THE COMMANDER OF THE LORD'S ARMY

As Joshua came near Jericho, he saw a man standing with a sword in his hand. The man told Joshua that he was the commander of the Lord's army and he had come to help Joshua. How do you think Joshua felt, knowing that he had a heavenly warrior on his side? Draw the sword in the hand of the Lord's commander.

Joshua went up to him and asked, "Are you for us or for our enemies?" Joshua 5:13

THE COMMANDER INSTRUCTS JOSHUA

The people of Jericho were afraid of the Israelite army because they had heard about the miracles that the Israelites' God had performed. The commander of the Lord's army told Joshua that Joshua would win the battle with Jericho. He even told him exactly how to attack! Joshua obeyed the commander's instructions and the Israelite army defeated Jericho.

Jericho was tightly shut up because of the Israelites.
No one went out and no one came in. Joshua 6:1

28

THE MARCH AROUND JERICHO

The Israelite army attacked Jericho by marching around the city for seven days while seven priests blew trumpets made of rams' horns. This was a strange way for an attack, but because the Israelites obeyed God's commands, Jericho's walls tumbled down. Draw a ram's horn trumpet for each priest.

All this time the trumpets were sounding. Joshua 6:9

SAMSON AND DELILAH

God gave Samson amazing strength to fight the Philistines. The Philistines wanted to know where Samson's power came from so they tricked him by offering money to Delilah to find out. Delilah pestered Samson until he told her that the secret was his long hair. While Samson slept, Delilah called a Philistine to shave his head. Samson was no longer strong. He was taken prisoner.

Having put him to sleep on her lap, she called a man to shave off the seven braids of his hair. Judges 16:19

SamSON aND the PillaRS

After Samson's head was shaved and all of his strength was gone, the Philistines blinded him and put him in prison. One day the rulers called him out of prison to entertain them in their pagan temple. No one realized that his strength had returned as his hair grew back. Crying out to God one last time for strength, Samson pushed down the pillars of the temple and the building collapsed, killing Samson and 3,000 Philistines. Draw hair, a moustache and a beard on Samson.

Then he pushed with all his might, and down came the temple on the rulers and all the people in it. Judges 16:30

HANNAH AND SAMUEL

Hannah prayed to God and promised Him that if she had a son, he would serve the Lord in the temple. After God gave her a son named Samuel, Hannah kept her promise to Him. When Samuel was a young boy, Hannah brought him to live in the temple to help Eli, the priest. As Eli's helper, Samuel was also God's helper. He grew up to be the greatest judge that Israel ever had.

I give him to the Lord. For his whole life he will be given over to the Lord. 1 Samuel 1:28

SAMUEL IN THE NIGHT

One night when Samuel was sleeping he heard his name called. He ran to Eli because he thought Eli called him. After Samuel heard his name called and ran to Eli three times, Eli realized the Lord was calling Samuel. The fourth time the Lord called Samuel, he was ready to hear what He had to say. Draw stars in the window and a candle on the table.

The Lord called Samuel a third time, and
Samuel got up and went to Eli. 1 Samuel 3:8

DAVID THE SHEPHERD

When David was young, he worked as a shepherd for his father's flocks. Shepherds lived day and night on the hillsides with their sheep. So much time alone allowed David to think about the Lord and the beauty of His creation. David played the harp. David wrote many of the Bible's psalms.

"There is still the youngest," Jesse answered,
"but he is tending the sheep." 1 Samuel 16:11

DaViD anD GOLiatH

The story of David and Goliath is a favorite of many. David had great courage to take on a giant. He was a young person who had faith in the Lord. God honored his faith and gave him the talent to defeat Goliath. Draw the giant Goliath.

The battle is the Lord's, and he will give all of you into our hands. 1 Samuel 17:47

DAVID AND JONATHAN

Jonathan was King Saul's son and a soldier in his father's army. David was a shepherd boy who proved himself a warrior by defeating Goliath. David and Jonathan became best friends. Jonathan was a true friend by helping David escape the anger of King Saul.

Jonathan took off the robe he was wearing and gave it to David, along with his tunic, and even his sword, his bow and his belt. 1 Samuel 18:4

36

David Shows Kindness

David loved Jonathan as if he were his own brother. Jonathan had a son named Mephibosheth, who could not walk well. After Jonathan died, David searched for Jonathan's son and brought him to his palace. At first Mephibosheth was afraid because he didn't know why David called for him. David wanted to show kindness toward his friend's son. He did so by inviting Mephibosheth and his family to eat at the king's table from that day on. Draw Mephibosheth's crutches lying on the floor beside him.

The king asked, "Is there no one still left of the house of Saul to whom I can show God's kindness?" 2 Samuel 9:3

THE PROPHETS OF BAAL ACCEPT A CHALLENGE

The people of Israel started to worship a false god named Baal. Elijah, the prophet of the one true God, wanted his people to see how wrong it was to worship Baal. So he challenged the people to make a sacrifice on their altar to their god. Elijah also would make a sacrifice, but his would be to the real God. Elijah said that the god who answered by sending fire to burn the sacrifice would surely be the most powerful. Baal's followers called and danced all day expecting to hear from Baal. But nothing happened, because he was not real.

They called on the name of Baal from morning till noon. 1 Kings 18:26

ELIJAH CALLS UPON GOD

Elijah knew that the false god Baal would not send fire to burn the sacrifice. He wanted to show Baal's followers the power of the real God. First, he set up an altar using 12 large stones with wood on top of the stones. Then he dug a huge ditch all the way around the altar. The sacrifice was placed on top of the wood. After that he ordered water to be poured over the entire altar and in the ditch. Finally, Elijah prayed to God. God sent fire to burn the sacrifice, wood, stones, water and even the dirt. The people saw who was the one and only true God! Draw fire coming down from heaven and burning up the altar.

Then the fire of the Lord fell and burned up the sacrifice. 1 Kings 18:38

Jezebel Seeks Elijah's Life

Jezebel was a very mean and wicked queen who served the false god Baal. Her husband was King Ahab, who was urged to do evil by his wife. Jezebel was angry that Elijah's God proved more powerful than Baal. She also was angry because Elijah had the false prophets put to death. She relied on these false prophets to make her rich. So Jezebel wanted to see Elijah put to death. She sent a messenger to tell Elijah that he would die the next day, just like Baal's prophets.

Now Ahab told Jezebel everything Elijah had done. 1 Kings 19:1

ELIJAH HIDES IN A MOUNTAIN

Elijah had proved how mighty God was by overcoming Baal's followers. Now Queen Jezebel was very angry and wanted Elijah killed. Elijah heard about this and ran far away from the queen to Mount Horeb, where he found a cave and spent the night. While Elijah was there, God told him to stand on the mountain. A great storm tore the mountain apart. But God was not in the storm. Then there was an earthquake and a fire, but God was not in those either. Finally, God spoke in a gentle whisper. Elijah realized he had to be quiet and listen for God, not just look for Him in mighty ways. Draw a great storm with dark clouds and lightning.

The Lord said, "Go out and stand on the mountain in the presence of the Lord."
1 Kings 19:11

THE FAITH OF A SERVANT GIRL

Naaman was a great army leader. He also had a terrible disease called leprosy, which could not be cured. Naaman's wife had a servant girl who heard about his disease. The servant girl knew of one of God's prophets, Elisha, who could heal Naaman. She told her mistress all about Elisha and the God he served. She had faith that God would help Elisha heal Naaman. The mistress told her husband the good news, and Naaman went in search of Elisha.

She said to her mistress, "If only my master would see the prophet who is in Samaria! He would cure him of his leprosy." 2 Kings 5:3

Naaman Obeys

Elisha, the prophet, heard that Naaman, the army captain, wanted to be healed of his leprosy. Elisha sent a message to Naaman telling him to wash seven times in the Jordan River, and he would be healed. Naaman was mad because the prophet did not even see him in person but just told him what to do in a letter. His servants finally convinced Naaman to go to the river. When he did as he was commanded, Naaman was healed. Naaman now had faith in God! Draw trees on the riverbanks.

So he went down and dipped himself in the Jordan seven times,
as the man of God had told him, and his flesh was restored. 2 Kings 5:14

SEARCH FOR A QUEEN

King Xerxes was searching for a beautiful, young girl to be his next queen. Esther was very pretty. She was brought to the king as one of the girls from whom he would choose for queen. The girls were taken into the king's palace and given beauty treatments before they were presented to the king. Esther was a Jew, one of God's people, but she did not tell anyone as her uncle Mordecai had instructed her. When the girls were presented to the king, he chose beautiful Esther, not knowing that she was a Jew.

Then let the girl who pleases the king be queen. Esther 2:4

THE QUEEN SAVES HER PEOPLE

Haman was a very bad man who talked the king into making a law that allowed Jews to be killed on a certain day. Mordecai, Queen Esther's uncle, told her about the law and begged her to talk to the king to stop it. Esther was a brave woman. She asked the king to save her and her people, the Jews. The king listened to Esther, and he stopped Haman's evil plan to kill the Jews. The king made another law that allowed the Jews to fight back. Esther helped save God's people, the Jews. Draw jewelry on Esther and stones in her crown.

Spare my people – this is my request. Esther 7:3

ORDERED TO WORSHIP AN IDOL

King Nebuchadnezzar of Babylon had his servants make a huge golden idol. It was 90 feet tall! The king called all of his people together to tell them about his new law. The new law said that any time music was played, all people must kneel and worship the idol. Whoever did not worship the idol would be thrown into a blazing furnace. There were many Jews who lived in Babylon. The Jews did not worship idols – they worshiped the one true God! The king heard about three Jews in particular – Shadrach, Meshach and Abednego – who were not obeying his law.

Whoever does not fall down and worship will immediately be thrown into a blazing furnace. Daniel 3:6

THROWN INTO A FURNACE

Shadrach, Meshach and Abednego refused to bow down to the king's golden idol. The king was angry! He had them thrown into a blazing furnace. The furnace was so hot that the soldiers who threw in the three men were killed by the blaze. But as the king looked at the furnace, he was surprised to see four men walking in it, not three! He called for Shadrach, Meshach and Abednego to come out of the blazing furnace. They came out completely unharmed by the fire. The Lord was the fourth person in the furnace, and He protected them. The king praised God because no other god had this kind of power. Draw fire in the furnace and smoke coming out of the chimneys.

These three men, firmly tied, fell into the blazing furnace. Daniel 3:23

DANIEL PRAYS

Daniel prayed a lot. Three times a day he would go home and pray to God. Some men who did not like Daniel talked the king into making a new law. This law said that anyone caught praying to God would be thrown into a den of lions. But this new law did not stop Daniel from praying.

These men went as a group and found Daniel praying and asking God for help. Daniel 6:11

DANIEL IN THE LIONS' DEN

Daniel was thrown into a lions' den because he refused to obey the king's new law that said he could not pray to God. The king liked Daniel and did not want to harm him, but when a law was made it had to be enforced. God was faithful to Daniel and sent an angel to shut the lions' mouths so no harm would be done to him. Draw closed mouths and whiskers on the lions.

When Daniel was lifted from the den, no wound was found on him, because he had trusted in his God. Daniel 6:23

JONAH ON BOARD

God told Jonah to go on a missionary trip to Nineveh. But Jonah decided to disobey God. He got on a boat that was headed far from Nineveh. He was trying to run away from God. A violent storm arose on the sea and the sailors decided that Jonah was the cause of the storm. They threw him overboard. The raging sea grew calm again. But God was not through with Jonah yet.

After paying the fare, he went aboard and sailed for Tarshish to flee from the Lord. Jonah 1:3

JONAH ON THE BEACH

Jonah was swallowed by a great fish after he was thrown overboard from the ship. He was in the fish's belly for three days and three nights. Jonah was sorry for disobeying God. He prayed to God and God heard his prayers. The great fish vomited Jonah onto the shore. Draw the great fish swimming away in the sea.

The Lord commanded the fish, and it vomited Jonah onto dry land. Jonah 2:10

ZECHARIAH AND ELIZABETH

Zechariah was a priest who worked in the temple serving God. He and his wife, Elizabeth, were very old and had no children. One day an angel told Zechariah that they would have a son who would serve God in a special way. This son, who would be known as John the Baptist, prepared people for the coming of Jesus.

They had no children, because Elizabeth was barren;
and they were both well along in years. Luke 1:7

JOSEPH AND MARY

God chose Mary and Joseph to be the mother and earthly father of His Son, Jesus. They were poor, ordinary people. Joseph was a carpenter and Mary was a young bride but God used them in His plan to send a Savior to the world. Draw some carpenter tools on the table, such as a hammer.

Joseph, the husband of Mary, of whom was born Jesus, who is called Christ. Matthew 1:16

JOHN THE BAPTIST

John the Baptist's life mission was to announce the coming of Jesus, the Messiah. John wore camel's hair clothing and ate locusts and wild honey. He preached and baptized people throughout the countryside of Judea. John baptized Jesus in the Jordan River. God was very pleased with Jesus – His Son – and John the Baptist.

As Jesus was coming up out of the water, he saw heaven being torn open and the Spirit descending on him like a dove. Mark 1:10

JOHN THE BAPTIST IN PRISON

John the Baptist spoke words of truth, which led people to repent of their sins. King Herod did not like when John the Baptist told him he was a sinner, so he put John in prison. King Herod's wife especially hated John. She had him killed. Draw the prison chains connecting John's wrists and ankles to the wall.

Herod himself had given orders to have John arrested, and he had him bound and put in prison. Mark 6:17

Jesus walks along the sea of Galilee

When Jesus began His ministry, He moved to Capernaum, a big town beside the Sea of Galilee. The Sea of Galilee is a large lake. Many men earned a living from fishing there. Walking along the sea was an ideal place to find fishermen, and that's exactly what Jesus did.

Jesus was walking beside the Sea of Galilee. Matthew 4:18

FISHERS OF MEN

As Jesus was walking along the Sea of Galilee, He saw Simon Peter and his brother Andrew fishing with nets. Jesus called them to follow Him. He said that He would make them fishers of men. So the brothers left their nets, boats and fish to follow Jesus. By being "fishers of men," they would now help to tell others about Jesus. Draw lots of fish in the net.

"Come, follow me," Jesus said, "and I will make you fishers of men." Matthew 4:19

WEDDING AT CANA

Jesus celebrated special events with His friends and family. He performed His first miracle at a wedding in a town called Cana. Jesus, His disciples and His mother were at this wedding and there was no more wine. When Jesus' mother heard about the wine, she asked Jesus to help.

When the wine was gone, Jesus' mother said to him, "They have no more wine." John 2:3

58

THE MIRACLE OF THE WINE

Jesus told the servants at the wedding in Cana to fill six large, empty stone jars with water. The servants then poured some and served it to the host of the wedding. It was no longer water but wine! It even tasted better than the wine they served before. This first miracle proved Jesus' power. When His disciples saw this, they believed in Him. Decorate the jars and draw water pouring out of the bucket.

Jesus said to the servants, "Fill the jars with water;" so they filled them to the brim. John 2:7

A DYING LITTLE GIRL

As Jesus traveled from town to town, many people crowded around Him, wanting to be healed. One day a man named Jairus came to Jesus and begged Him to come to his house. He said his only daughter, who was 12 years old, was dying. Jairus knew Jesus could heal her. He loved her very much. But as Jesus was traveling to Jairus' house, someone told him that Jairus' daughter had died already. It was too late for Jesus...or so they thought!

A man named Jairus...came and fell at Jesus' feet, pleading with him to come to his house because his only daughter...was dying. Luke 8:41-42

A LITTLE GIRL IS ALIVE

Jesus went immediately to Jairus' house, even though the little girl had just died. Her family was crying because they were very sad that she died. Jesus told them not to worry. He said she was not dead, only asleep. They laughed at Him because they knew she was not asleep. Jesus went into her room, took her by the hand and told her to get up. And she did just that! Jesus brought her back to life! Jairus and the girl's mother were amazed at the miracle, and they believed in Jesus. Draw a pillow on the little girl's bed.

Her spirit returned, and at once she stood up. Luke 8:55

zacchaeus in the crowd

Everywhere Jesus went He was followed by crowds of people. When Jesus came to Jericho, a man named Zacchaeus could not see Him because he was short. He had heard so much about Jesus, though, that he had to find a way to see Him. But the crowds would not budge, so he ran ahead and climbed a sycamore tree, where he waited for the Lord to come by.

He wanted to see who Jesus was, but being a short man
he could not, because of the crowd. Luke 19:3

ZACCHAEUS IN THE TREE

As Jesus was walking with the crowd in Jericho, He came to the sycamore tree where Zacchaeus was. Jesus looked up and called Zacchaeus to come down at once because He was going to his house that very day! The crowd complained because Zacchaeus was a tax collector who got rich by cheating them. After meeting Jesus, Zacchaeus' heart changed. Draw Zacchaeus' money bag tied around his waist.

*So he ran ahead and climbed a sycamore-fig tree to see him,
since Jesus was coming that way.* Luke 19:4

63

FRIENDS CARRY A MAN ON A COT

Jesus went from town to town preaching and healing people. One day when He was preaching at a home in Capernaum, there was such a huge crowd that it was hard to get near Jesus. Four men who heard of Jesus' healing power came carrying a crippled friend on a mat. When the friends saw the crowd they did not get discouraged but instead looked for another way to get to Jesus.

So many gathered that there was no room left, not even outside the door. Mark 2:2

SICK MAN IS LOWERED THROUGH ROOF

The four friends of the crippled man had faith that Jesus could heal him. Since they could not get through the crowd they decided to take him to the roof. Houses in Bible times were built with flat roofs made of mud and straw. It was easy for the friends to make a hole in the roof and lower the crippled man to Jesus. The crippled man was healed because of their faith in Jesus. Draw ropes coming from the hole in the ceiling to the handles on the mat.

Since they could not get him to Jesus be
they made an opening in the roof above Jesu
through it, lowered the mat the paralyzed man wa

JESUS ASLEEP ON THE BOAT

One day Jesus and His disciples got into a boat and headed for the other side of the Sea of Galilee. Jesus fell asleep as they sailed. Suddenly a violent storm arose and water gushed into the boat. The disciples were in danger of drowning.

d, he fell asleep. A squall came down on the lake, so that the
ing swamped, and they were in great danger. Luke 8:23

JESUS CALMS THE SEA

The disciples were afraid. They panicked as the storm raged around them. Jesus was unconcerned about the danger because He was sleeping. Finally, the disciples called out to Him to save them. Jesus stood up and immediately calmed the sea by His command. The disciples were amazed that all of nature obeyed Jesus. Draw the calm sea, the shining sun and clouds in the sky.

He got up and rebuked the wind and the raging waters;
the storm subsided, and all was calm. Luke 8:24

JESUS VISITS MARY AND MARTHA

Mary and Martha were sisters who both loved Jesus very much. They also had a brother named Lazarus. Jesus often visited them at their home. They were wonderful hosts and they welcomed Jesus with open arms.

He came to a village where a woman named Martha opened her home to him. Luke 10:38

MARTHA COMPLAINS TO JESUS

After Jesus entered Mary and Martha's home, Mary sat at Jesus' feet to listen to everything He had to say. Martha got busy right away with cooking. She soon realized that she was doing all of the work while her sister was doing nothing! She complained to Jesus, who corrected her. Martha was so busy doing things to please people that she forgot Jesus. Draw bowls on the table and a fire under the pot.

She came to him and asked, "Lord, don't you care that my sister has left me to do the work by myself? Tell her to help me!" Luke 10:40

69

A WOMAN AT THE WELL

While Jesus was traveling through the country of Samaria, He stopped at a well to rest. In Bible times, people got their drinking water from a well and they had to carry it home in large jugs. Around noon, a woman came to the well to get water. Jesus asked her to give Him a drink. She was surprised that He spoke to her because men did not talk to women in those days, especially a Samaritan. Jews did not talk to Samaritans. Jesus told her He could give her a special kind of water and she would never get thirsty again. The woman was curious. She wanted to learn more about this water.

A Samaritan woman came to draw water. John 4:7

LIVING WATER

Jesus offered the woman at the well "living water" so that she would never be "thirsty" again. She didn't understand at first, but Jesus was talking about Himself. Jesus is the One who can make us happy! Jesus also told her about the bad things she had done in her life, and she was amazed that He knew. She finally realized that Jesus was the Messiah. She left her jar at the well and ran into the town to tell others that she had just met Jesus, the Savior. Draw a jug of water on the well.

The woman said to him, "Sir, give me this water so that I won't get thirsty." John 4:15

Teaching the Multitude

It was difficult for Jesus and His disciples to get away by themselves without interruptions. One day over 5,000 people followed Jesus because they had heard about His miraculous healing power. He could have sent them all away, but instead He gladly welcomed them. Jesus loved and cared for them.

He welcomed them and spoke to them about the kingdom of God,
and healed those who needed healing. Luke 9:11

FEEDING THE MULTITUDE

It was getting late in the day as Jesus preached and healed. The disciples became worried about what the people would eat since there were so many. They wanted to send them all home but Jesus had another plan. He took a boy's five bread loaves and two fish and miraculously fed over 5,000 people! Draw the five bread loaves and the two fish in the boy's basket.

Another of his disciples, Andrew, Simon Peter's brother, spoke up, "Here is a boy with five small barley loaves and two small fish, but how far will they go among so many?" John 6:8

MARTHA RUNS TO MEET JESUS

Mary and Martha sent word to Jesus in another town that their brother Lazarus was very sick and needed healing. Jesus, who loved Lazarus, did not rush to heal him, but instead waited two more days before He went. Martha ran to meet Jesus when she heard He was finally coming but it was too late because Lazarus was already dead. Martha and Mary could not understand why Jesus was not there when they needed Him.

"Lord," Martha said to Jesus, "if you had been here,
my brother would not have died." John 11:21

Jesus Raises Lazarus From the Dead

Mary and Martha took Jesus to the tomb where Lazarus' body was placed. Jesus had the huge stone in front of the tomb moved away. After praying to God, He called in a loud voice, "Lazarus, come out!" To everyone's amazement, Lazarus came out alive! Many of the Jews with Mary and Martha put their faith in Jesus after seeing this. Draw the huge stone that was moved away from the tomb.

The dead man came out, his hands and feet wrapped with strips of linen, and a cloth around his face. John 11:44

THE TRIUMPHAL ENTRY

When the great Feast of Passover was about to begin, Jesus rode into Jerusalem on a donkey. People heard that He was coming so they took palm branches and shouted, "Blessed is the King who comes in the name of the Lord!" They wanted Jesus to be the king and ruler of their land. They did not understand that He wanted to be the King and Ruler of their hearts.

*Many people spread their cloaks on the road,
while others spread branches they had cut in the fields.* Mark 11:8

THE UPPER ROOM

When the Feast of Passover arrived, Jesus sent Peter and John to make the preparations. Unleavened bread, wine and herbs were bought, as well as a lamb to cook. Jesus told them to go to Jerusalem where a man carrying water would meet them and take them to a large upstairs room where they would eat the Passover meal. The disciples did as Jesus said and prepared the meal. Draw a window in the upstairs room.

He will show you a large upper room, all furnished. Make preparations there. Luke 22:12

THE LAST SUPPER

The Passover meal was the last meal Jesus ate before He was crucified. He and His disciples ate it in the upstairs room that was furnished for the occasion. While they ate, Jesus told them that one of them would soon betray Him and one would deny Him. This was hard for the disciples to understand, but Jesus knew what the next several hours would bring — His own cruel death on a cross.

And he said to them,
"I have eagerly desired to eat this Passover with you before I suffer." Luke 22:15

THE GARDEN OF GETHSEMANE

In the evening after the Passover meal, Jesus and His disciples went to the Garden of Gethsemane. Jesus went ahead of the disciples and prayed alone. When He came back to them, He found them sleeping instead of keeping watch and praying. Jesus was suffering terrible agony because He knew what was going to happen to Him, yet He was willing to suffer in order to save us from our sins. Draw trees, flowers, stars and a moon.

And being in anguish, he prayed more earnestly,
and his sweat was like drops of blood falling to the ground. Luke 22:44

79

THE CRUCIFIXION

Jesus was nailed to a wooden cross for all to see. Many had come to watch the crucifixion, including Jesus' mother. Some who watched yelled insults at Him. Some were deeply saddened. There were two criminals nailed to crosses beside Jesus. One criminal mocked Him, but the other one recognized Him as the Son of God who had done nothing to deserve His punishment.

Near the cross of Jesus stood his mother. John 19:25

THE GARDEN TOMB

The greatest news ever proclaimed to the world was the angel's announcement that Jesus had risen from the dead. When the women went to the tomb early in the morning with burial spices, an angel announced, "He is not here. He has risen, just as He said. Come and see the place where He lay." Most of the Jews and the Roman government thought that killing Jesus would put an end to His influence on people. Little did they know that Jesus' death on the cross was just the beginning. Draw flowers and a rising sun coming up behind the hills.

At the place where Jesus was crucified, there was a garden, and in the garden a new tomb, in which no one had ever been laid. They laid Jesus there. John 19:41-42

Breakfast By the Sea

After Jesus rose from the dead, He appeared to many people at different times. On one occasion, Jesus had breakfast prepared for His disciples on the seashore. They had been fishing in a boat all night without any luck. Jesus called out and told them to throw their net on the right side of their boat. When they did this, they had so many fish that it was difficult to haul them in. The disciples then realized that it was Jesus who was calling to them. They went ashore immediately and had breakfast with Him.

When they landed, they saw a fire of burning coals there
with fish on it, and some bread. John 21:9

THE ASCENSION

After His resurrection, Jesus appeared to His disciples on a mountaintop. He told them to go into the world and teach people about the good news of Jesus Christ, making them disciples and baptizing them. He promised them that He would be with them always. His commands were not just for the disciples but for us, too. Jesus wants us to tell people about Him so they will have a chance to be saved. Draw the clouds around Jesus as He goes up to heaven.

After the Lord Jesus had spoken to them, he was taken up into heaven. Mark 16:19

THE CHURCH BEGINS

After Jesus was crucified, His disciples were afraid. So after He rose from the dead, Jesus came back to earth and spent 40 days with the disciples. When Jesus left the second time, the disciples were brave and ready to tell others about Him. Jesus had taught them about God's kingdom. They knew He was real and everything He said was true. But before Jesus went up to heaven, He told His disciples to wait in Jerusalem. A special gift from God was coming their way.

He appeared to them over a period of forty days and spoke about the kingdom of God.
Acts 1:3

THE HOLY SPIRIT COMES TO A SECRET ROOM

God's gift of the Holy Spirit came, just as Jesus promised. A group of Christians were gathered in a house when suddenly a sound like a terrible storm filled the whole place. Then they saw what looked like tongues of fire coming from heaven and landing on each one of them. (It wasn't really fire, because no one was burned – it only looked like fire!) The people realized that God had given them this Spirit and that with the Spirit's help they could begin the job of spreading the Good News of Jesus. Draw tongues of fire coming down and landing on the people.

They saw what seemed to be tongues of fire that separated and came to rest on each of them. Acts 2:3

PETER AND JOHN GO TO PRAY

Peter and John had a mission: to tell people about Jesus. Sometimes the Holy Spirit gave the apostles power to heal so those people would believe in Jesus. One day as Peter and John were walking to the temple to pray, they met a man who had never been able to walk. He had to beg for money every day because he could not work to earn money as other people could. Peter and John had no money to give the man, but they had something even better.

One day Peter and John were going up to the temple at the time of prayer. Acts 3:1

PeTer Heals a Crippled Beggar

The crippled beggar asked Peter and John for money as they walked by. Instead, God worked through Peter to give the man something even more valuable – the ability to walk! Peter took the man by the hand and the man stood up on both feet. The man was so happy that he went jumping for joy and praising God. He wouldn't have to beg or have other people carry him around anymore. The town's people were amazed. Draw a happy face on the beggar, and sandals on his feet.

He jumped to his feet and began to walk. Acts 3:8

ANANIAS LIES TO GOD

The first Christians shared everything they had with each other. No one needed anything. Some of the Christians even sold their land and gave the money to the apostles. Ananias and Sapphira were a married couple who sold their land and said they would give all the money from it to the apostles. But Ananias decided to keep some of the money for himself. He lied – not only to the apostles but also to God. When Peter asked Ananias about it, Ananias fell down and died.

You have not lied to men but to God. Acts 5:4

SAPPHIRA LIES TO GOD

Several hours later, Sapphira went to see the apostles. She didn't know what had happened to Ananias. The apostles asked if the money they received for the land was correct. Sapphira knew in her heart it was not, but she lied and said yes anyway. Just like her husband, who also lied, she died because of her sin. Draw a money bag in Sapphira's hand.

About three hours later his wife came in, not knowing what had happened. Acts 5:7

DORCAS IS LOVED BY MANY

Dorcas was a woman who did kind deeds for other people. One of the deeds was making clothing for the poor. One day when Peter was in Joppa, where Dorcas lived, he heard that she had died. Peter knew Dorcas' friends were very sad that she died and that they were going to miss her very much. When Peter arrived at Dorcas's house, he had everyone leave the room where she lay. Peter got down on his knees and prayed. Suddenly, Dorcas came to life and sat up!

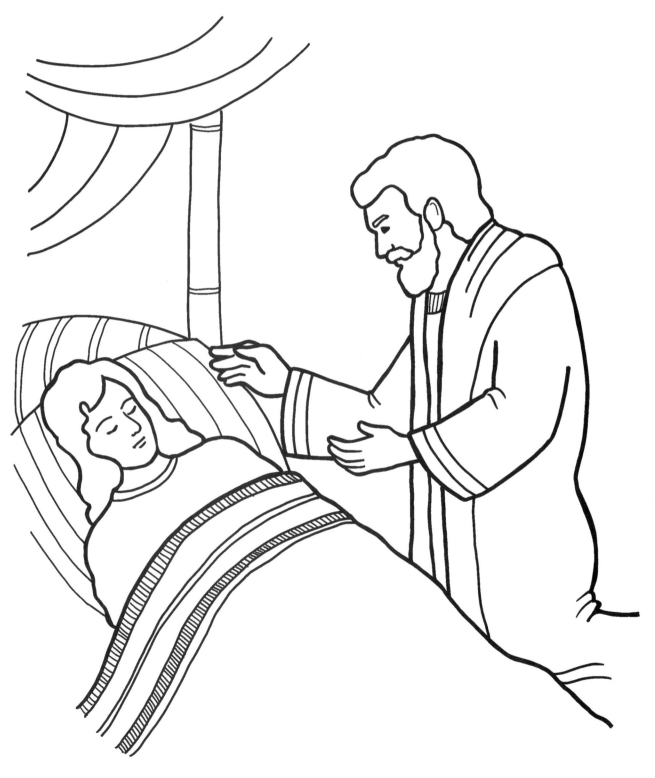

She opened her eyes, and seeing Peter she sat up. Acts 9:40

PETER HEALS DORCAS

God helped Peter bring Dorcas back from the dead. Many people believed in Jesus because of this miracle. Dorcas was kind, and she had a lot of friends. She made robes for friends, and for people who had no clothing. Decorate the robe that Dorcas made.

All the widows stood around him, crying and showing him the robes and other clothing that Dorcas had made. Acts 9:39

PETER KNOCKS ON THE DOOR

Peter was arrested and put in prison for telling people about Jesus. While Peter was in prison, the church people prayed for his release. God answered their prayers and sent an angel to Peter. The angel led Peter past the guards, through the gate and out into the city. Peter then went to Mary's house, where many people were praying for him. He knocked on the door but the servant girl didn't let him in at first. She couldn't believe it was Peter! The people in the house didn't believe it was Peter because they thought he was still in prison.

But Peter kept on knocking. Acts 12:16

PETER ENTERS MARY'S HOUSE

Peter kept knocking on the door until the people in Mary's house finally let him in. They were very excited and happy to see him, and amazed that their prayers were answered so quickly. But Peter quieted them down and then told them how the Lord led him to safety. Back at the prison, the guards had no idea what happened to Peter. King Herod searched everywhere for him but Peter was safe at Mary's house. Many more people believed in Jesus because of this miraculous escape. Draw wood on the door and a curtain on the window.

Peter motioned with his hand for them to be quiet and described how the Lord had brought him out of prison. Acts 12:17

LYDIA BELIEVES IN JESUS

The apostles were not allowed to hold prayer meetings in the city of Philippi, so they went to the river to pray. Once they got to the river, they sat down and spoke about Jesus to the women who were gathered there. Lydia was one of the women. She sold purple cloth for a living, and she was very wealthy. But even though she was wealthy, she still needed Jesus. Her heart was opened to Paul's teaching. She believed in Jesus and was baptized in the river along with the rest of her family.

One of those listening was a woman named Lydia. Acts 16:14

LYDIA SHARES WITH MISSIONARIES

Paul, Silas, Timothy and Luke were missionaries who took the Gospel of Jesus throughout the world. They didn't have hotels like we have today, so they had to rely on other Christians for beds and food. Lydia was a Christian who invited them into her home. She gave them a place to sleep, good food and friendship. In return, Lydia was blessed because she and her family got to hear more about Jesus while the missionaries were there. Draw fruit on the table.

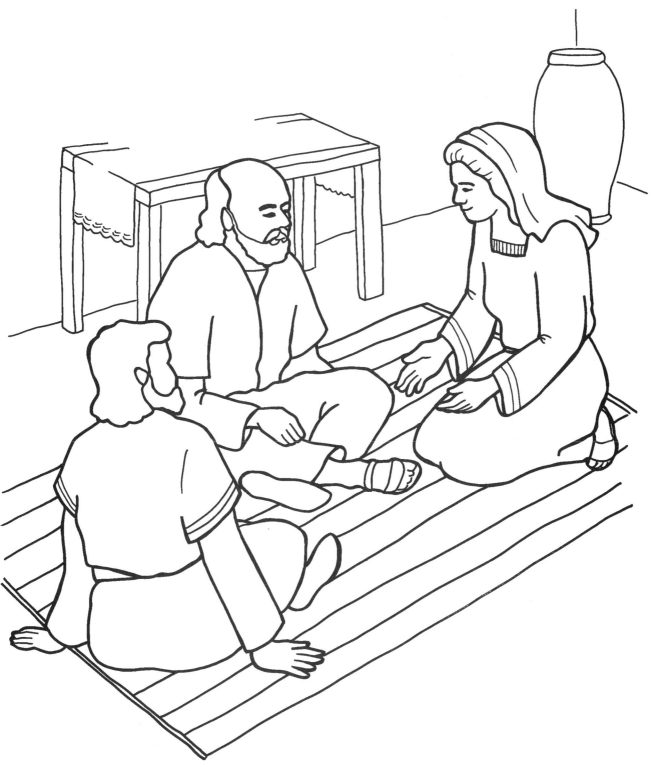

"If you consider me a believer in the Lord," she said, *"come and stay at my house."*
Acts 16:15